KIDS THROUGHOUT HISTORY™

Kids During the Renaissance

Lisa A. Wroble

The Rosen Publishing Group's
PowerKids Press™
New York

Published in 1997 by The Rosen Publishing Group, Inc.
29 East 21st Street, New York, NY 10010

First Edition

Book Design: Danielle Primiceri

Photo Credits: Cover © Corbis-Bettmann; p. 4 by Filippino Lippi, provided by Corbis-Bettmann; p. 7 provided by The Bettmann Archive; p. 8 by Michelangelo Merisi Caravaggio, provided by The Bettmann Archive; p. 11 by Jan Steer, provided by Bettmann; p. 12 by Jan Vermeer, provided by Bettmann; p. 15 by Pieter Brueghel, provided by Bettmann; p. 16 by David Teniers, provided by The Bettmann Archive; p. 19 provided by Archive Photos; p. 20 by Donati Creti, provided by Bettmann.

Wroble, Lisa A.
    Kids during the Renaissance / Lisa A. Wroble.
        p.   cm.—(Kids throughout history)
    Includes index.
    ISBN 0-8239-5121-9
    1. Renaissance—Juvenile literature.2 Children—Italy—History—Juvenile literature. 3. Renaissance—Italy—Juvenile literature. I. Title. II. Series: Wroble, Lisa A. Kids throughout history.
    GT130.W76 1997
    305.23'094'09024—dc21   96-48777
                                                               CIP
                                                               AC r97

Manufactured in the United States of America

Contents

A Time of Rebirth

The **Renaissance** (REN-uh-sahnts) was an exciting time in history. It was a time of great change. The word "renaissance" means "rebirth." During this time there was a lot of interest in learning new things. The Renaissance lasted from the 1300s to the early 1600s. It began in Italy, and soon grew to include the rest of Europe. **Trade** (TRAYD) between cities grew. Cities and countries became larger. People studied math, science, art, music, and medicine in new ways.

The Renaissance affected people in cities all over Europe. Children had more opportunities than ever before.

A Renaissance City

Isabella and her brother, Stefano, lived in Venice, a city in northern Italy. Venice had a **seaport** (SEE-port) where ships came and went. Many ships carried goods that were made in Italy, such as lace and fabric, to countries around the world. Other ships brought **imported** (im-POR-ted) goods, such as spices, from other countries. Isabella's father was a **merchant** (MER-chent). He brought many different goods to Venice. Then he sold them throughout the rest of Italy.

During the Renaissance, some people became wealthy by trading goods with other countries. ▶

Daily Life

Isabella and her family lived in a house near the seaport. Her house had many rooms. Isabella's favorite room was the big kitchen. She learned to cook, clean, and sew from watching and helping her mother. Isabella and her mother went to the market every day. They bought vegetables, bread, and fish or meat for their meals. **Vendors** (VEN-derz) that sold the same kinds of things, such as fish or meat, were in the same area. That area was often named after whatever was sold there.

◄ *There were no supermarkets during the Renaissance. People went to different vendors to buy different foods.*

Clothing

During the Renaissance, children dressed the same way as grown-ups. Many people during the Renaissance wore bright, colorful clothes. Some people's clothes were made of silk and lace. Boys and men wore leggings called hose. They also wore **tunics** (TOO-niks). Wealthy men wore tunics trimmed with fur. Over their tunics they wore capes.

Girls and women wore gowns with belts just above the waist. Many women wore wide headbands called snoods to hold their hair away from their faces.

Children were dressed like little grown-ups. ▶

Education

During the Renaissance, most children started school when they were seven years old. Like most girls, Isabella stopped going to school once she had learned to read. She finished her schooling at home. There she studied the Bible and other books. Some boys usually finished their education at a **university** (yoo-nih-VER-sih-tee).

Some parents could only afford to send their sons to school to learn to read. Then the boys had to learn skills for a job. The girls stayed home and learned to keep house.

Many girls finished their education at home. Some girls learned to play musical instruments, such as the piano.

Free-Time Fun

When Isabella was finished with her chores, she and her friends often played with marbles or dolls. Sometimes they made mud pies or gathered seashells. Sometimes they played a game very much like tag. Afterwards, the kids would gather around a grown-up and listen to stories that were read out loud. Isabella loved to **recite** (ree-SYT) poetry, sing, and dance with her friends. Many children had pets. Isabella had a **cricket** (KRIH-ket) that she kept in a pretty cage.

Kids during the Renaissance played many of the same games that kids play today. ▶

Carnival

Many people who lived during the Renaissance were **Christian** (KRIS-chen). For six weeks before Easter, Christians prayed and often ate very little. This time was called Lent. To get ready for Lent, most cities held a big celebration called **Carnival** (KAR-nih-vul). During Carnival, many people wore fancy costumes and masks. Banners were hung from windows. Isabella loved to watch people act out scenes from history and from the Bible.

◄ *People sang and danced in the streets during Carnival.*

Science

During the Renaissance, great thinkers began learning things in new ways. Before the Renaissance, many people had just believed what they were told. Now scientists studied more to find out if what they were told was true or not. Sometimes it was true. But more often, it was not. An **astronomer** (uh-STRON-uh-mer) named Galileo discovered that the sun did not move around Earth, as everyone had always thought. In fact, Earth moves around the sun.

For a long time, people didn't believe what Galileo said about the sun and Earth. ▶
But he was right.

Art and Music

Isabella noticed that the art from her time looked different from the art that was painted earlier. That was because Renaissance artists began to create art that looked more realistic than it had before.

Even Renaissance music was different. Before, most music had been written for singers. But now flutes and pianos replaced the singers. Isabella was learning how to play the piano.

People met and played music in the room of someone's home. This was called chamber music. People still listen to chamber music today.

Modern Times

The Renaissance was the beginning of a time in which people looked at the world in new ways. The spirit of questioning things opened the door to many discoveries in art, science, medicine, and many other areas. We have the people of the Renaissance to thank for so many of the ways we look at and do things in **modern** (MAH-dern) times.

Glossary

astronomer (uh-STRON-uh-mer) Someone who studies the sun, moon, stars, and planets.

Carnival (KAR-nih-vul) Festival held before Easter.

Christian (KRIS-chen) Believing in Jesus Christ.

cricket (KRIH-ket) A small, winged insect.

import (im-PORT) To bring in from another country.

merchant (MER-chent) A person who buys and sells goods for a living.

modern (MAH-dern) Of the present time.

recite (ree-SYT) To repeat from memory.

Renaissance (REN-uh-sahnts) A time in history of new ideas and new ways of learning.

seaport (SEE-port) A port or harbor on the coast of a sea.

trade (TRAYD) A job that involves buying and selling goods.

tunic (TOO-nik) A piece of clothing like a long shirt.

university (yoo-nih-VER-sih-tee) A place of higher learning.

vendor (VEN-der) A person who sells something.

23

Index

4-75